The Hungry Kitten's Tale

Written by Elizabeth Fust
Illustrated by Mary MacArthur

The Hungry Kitten's Tale

Copyright © 2019 Elizabeth Fust

No part of this work may be reproduced in any form or by any electronic or mechanical means, including information storage and retrieval systems, without written permission in writing from the author, except brief quotations for review purposes.

Editing and book design by Jansina of Rivershore Books
Illustrations by Mary MacArthur

Age range: 4–10 years

ISBN: 978-1-63522-204-3

Printed in the United States of America
10   9   8   7   6   5   4   3   2

Rivershore Books
8982 Van Buren St. NE • Minneapolis, MN 55434
763-670-8677 • info@rivershorebooks.com

Many cats lived in the small town of Bethsaida. Some lived with families and caught mice, some lived with important people and lounged on cushions all day, and some wandered the streets with nowhere to go and no food for supper. Kit was one of those cats.

Bethsaida was a desert-like place and not much food grew there. There were many cows, but their milk was saved by the farmers, not given to stray cats like Kit.

It was not a very exciting place for a cat. That is, until one day a man visited Bethsaida. That man was followed by twelve others, and then by five thousand people! The man spoke to them all day about a kingdom of a king named God; it sounded like a wonderful place filled with nice people, the kind of people who are good to each other and to cats.

Kit hoped that someone in the crowd listening to the man had brought some food and would give some to him. But none of them did. In fact, not one of them had food!

One of the twelve went to his friend who had led them and said, "Should we tell the people to go find somewhere else to buy dinner? There is no food in Bethsaida."

The friend replied, "Let's give them the food we have."

"We don't have any food," one of the twelve said.

"Then we'll go find some," the friend told him.

Kit followed the men as they went around Bethsaida. They went to the farmers, the fishermen, and the important people. But no one had food for them.

They sadly made their way back and Kit followed, just as sad as they were. But then Kit smelled something. Barley bread and fish!

A boy with a basket sat by the side of the road with his head in his hands. Kit sniffed the basket and climbed in; inside were five loaves of bread and two fish! So much food for a cat, but not enough for the crowd, Kit thought.

"Why are you sad?" One of the men asked the boy after he had seen Kit go to him.

"I have been trying to sell bread baked by my mother and fish caught by my father to make money for my family. But no one will buy them because it isn't the nicest looking bread or the best catch of fish."

Kit wasn't listening to the boy. He reached a paw out to snatch a fish, but the man lifted Kit out of the basket. "We will buy it."

The men took the basket back to their friend. Kit and the boy followed them.

"Master, we only found five loaves of bread and two fish. There is no way we can feed everyone."

Which is what Kit had thought, too.

The friend said, "Bring me the food and have everyone sit down."

Kit sat next to the boy. He was still hoping someone would give him something to eat.

The leader of the twelve took the food and looked up to the heavens. Kit looked, too, but there were no birds flying in the sky so he didn't know what was so interesting that the man saw. But the man holding the fish and bread was interesting, so Kit watched him. The man said a blessing over the food. Then he broke off some bread for himself and passed it to his friends. Each of his friends broke off a piece and then continued passing it around to the people gathered there.

Kit got up and followed the food as it passed from hand to hand in the crowd. It seemed no matter how much bread or fish was eaten, it did not run out! The people were messy and dropped food everywhere, so Kit ran around gobbling it up. It was the best bread and the best fish he had ever tasted!

After eating, the five thousand people all wandered away to rest after their big dinner. Kit was so sleepy from eating so much good food, too. He went back to the boy's basket by the man and his friends.

The man told his friends to go pick up the leftover food and put it into baskets. Kit helped for a while, but then he climbed into the boy's basket and fell asleep.

"Master!" someone said, waking Kit up. "We filled twelve baskets of barley bread and fish! But the boy only had five loaves of bread and two fish. How can this be?"

The man smiled. "When my people are hungry, I will give them food. Boy, take these baskets of food, sell some of it for money for your family, and eat the rest for dinner."

"Thank you!" The boy started to pick up some baskets. He picked up the one Kit was in.

"Master! There's a cat in my basket!"

The man picked Kit up and rubbed his head until Kit couldn't stop purring. "Why don't you take him home? He can help you take care of your family, and eat your leftover fish, too."

He handed Kit to the boy. The boy smiled at Kit and gave him some fish. Kit liked him already. The boy placed Kit on his shoulder, picked up the baskets of bread and fish, and started walking home to his family. But then he stopped and turned to the man.

"Master, thank you for these gifts. Who are you?"

The man smiled at the boy and Kit. "My name is Jesus of Nazareth. Go in peace."

Then Jesus turned and started walking to the mountains by the sea.

Kit watched Jesus as he grew smaller and smaller in the distance. What an interesting and kind man! Kit couldn't wait to be a house cat, with a boy for a friend and supper every day. But he would never forget Jesus, who had used five loaves of bread and two fish to feed five thousand people—and one little cat.

Elizabeth Fust
(Author)

According to her mom, Elizabeth wrote her first story before she had even started school. She grew up in Michigan and the more she grew up the farther up north she moved, now she lives in the Upper Peninsula because it is always nice to read on a beach or write stories on your front porch. Elizabeth has been writing and reading for a long time because she enjoys it and she hopes you will enjoying reading her book!

Mary MacArthur
(Illustrator)

Mary MacArthur is an illustrator and comics artist. She was born, grew up, and went to art school in Texas, spending summers in Minnesota, where she now lives. She may not be a cat person, but she has one to keep the mice away and to model for illustrations like these.

Acknowledgements

Thank you to my friends who helped me write this book...

Thanks to Jansina of Rivershore Books. A writer couldn't ask for a better publisher, mentor, and friend!

Thanks to Mary MacArthur for sharing your talents to illustrate my story. It couldn't come alive without your drawings!

Thanks to the friends who gave me feedback as this book was being created. I couldn't have done this without you, Elizabeth Bertucci, Emily Langlois, Kendra Youren, and Julia Hoving!

And thanks to all the friends and family who have supported me throughout the years in all my writing endeavors!

Rivershore Books

www.rivershorebooks.com
info@rivershorebooks.com
www.facebook.com/rivershore.books
www.twitter.com/rivershorebooks
blog.rivershorebooks.com
forum.rivershorebooks.com

www.ingramcontent.com/pod-product-compliance
Lightning Source LLC
Chambersburg PA
CBHW041108070526
44583CB00002B/111